CAREER AS A

PHOTOGRAPHER

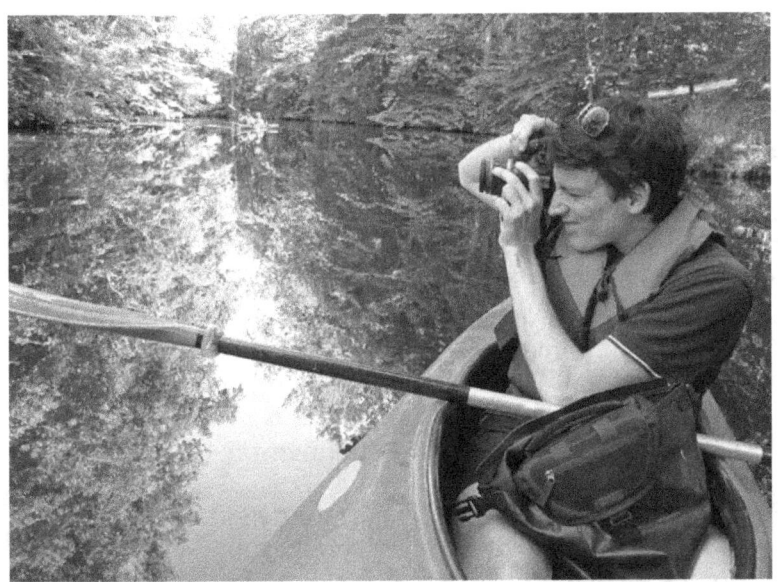

PHOTOGRAPHERS CAPTURE A MOMENT, preserve a memory that will last forever. With the push of a button, the click of the camera, a blink of an eye, you either succeed in your job or you fail. In many cases, there are no do-overs. If you miss the shot, it is gone forever. That is what makes you a professional – you do not miss the picture of a lifetime. It is sharp, vivid, and perfectly framed.

Photography is an art form. You create a style of your own, a way of taking pictures that is distinctively yours. You leave an imprint on every photograph you take. Your work stands on its own, speaks for itself. The lens becomes an extension of your eye. Few careers offer the opportunity to bring such a measure of individuality to a job. What you see through that camera lens is exclusively yours. Those who pick up a camera for a living have to be committed; they have to be driven. The dedication to produce a great photo can never leave you. It takes much more than a casual interest to succeed as a professional photographer, and your passion has to be reflected in your work.

Getting a great photograph is painstaking work. You must have expertise in using the best photographic equipment and then you have to work wonders with that gear.

You will have pressure in this profession. Some comes with the job, some you put on yourself because you know what you can do and expect only the best from yourself. Consider the nature photographer who is sent on assignment to get rare photos of a hard-to-find and difficult-to-approach species of animal. These could be the only photos taken of these particular animals for decades. It is literally the chance of a lifetime, a make-or-break assignment.

Photographers put in years honing their skills. When they are not out on assignment, they are busy perfecting their technique. Reaching new heights is what makes this career so challenging and keeps it fresh and exciting. Photographers are always pursuing that next great photo, and what adds to the thrill is you never know when and where you will come across it.

The rewards of the photographer's life are many. Great photographs appear in museums, exhibit halls, magazines, books, publications of all kinds, on television, on the Internet, and in the homes of wealthy collectors.

WHAT YOU CAN DO NOW

DO YOU REALLY LOVE TO TAKE PICTURES? Professional photographers rarely put down their cameras. Everything they see, everywhere they go, can be a photo opportunity.

If you are that committed to a career capturing life through a camera lens, learn everything you can about photography. The best way to do that is by finding someone in your area who is a professional photographer, and who may be interested in becoming your mentor. A mentor can help you learn how to use photographic equipment properly and critique all aspects of your photographic work. You should be able to learn something from every photograph you take. In that way, each time you take pictures your work improves and you grow in your craft.

You will find photography clubs in schools and in your community. There you can meet people who share your passion for photography and can help you learn new techniques and expand your horizons.

School and community newspapers are always looking for exceptional photographs to go along with stories in their publications, and this is a way to get your work in print and seen by others. School yearbooks are a good showcase for your work as well, and will give you plenty of opportunities to take both set-up and candid shots. These early forays into photography will give you a chance to develop your own photographic style. If you are lucky, your name will appear alongside your photo, giving you credit for your work.

HISTORY OF THE CAREER

IN 1839, WHEN THE PROCESS known as photography was introduced to the world, it was more than amazing; it was practically considered a miracle. People believed photography gave them the chance to go back in time, relive a moment, see friends and family members at their best, and preserve history.

Early photographic processes – daguerreotype and calotype – were quite complicated. The equipment and materials needed to produce those photos were expensive, bulky, and heavy to carry around. None of that dampened the public's enthusiasm for having a picture of the family to pass down through the generations. Even with all the drawbacks, intrepid pioneers learned the intricate process of taking pictures and set up studios to handle the demand for pictures from people all over the world.

By 1841, there were photography studios in major cities in France and England, and entrepreneurs started opening photo shops throughout the United States as well. One of the pioneers of professional photography in America was John Plumbe Jr, a civil engineer and railroad surveyor turned photo buff. Plumbe traveled quite a bit for his job. In early March 1840, Plumbe was in Boston and met Francois Gouraud. Gouraud had ventured to the states from France to promote daguerreotype. Louis Jacques Mande Daguerre invented that photographic process in France. Plumbe spent the next few months learning all he could about daguerreotype and by the end of the year he opened a photography studio in Washington, DC.

By 1845, Plumbe had opened 25 studios throughout the country. That same year the enterprising photographer took the first picture ever of a sitting president, James K. Polk. It was Plumbe who is credited with taking some of the earliest photographs of historic buildings in Washington, DC and getting those sites global recognition by sending the pictures worldwide. Those structures included the White House and the Capitol Building.

As Plumbe was opening his studios, inventors were refining the photographic process to make taking pictures easier and more practical. That helped open the profession to more up-and-coming photographers.

In 1844, Mathew Brady, who would become one of the nation's foremost photographers, launched his career by opening his first studio in New York City. Brady was only 21 years old at the time. Brady counted among his clientele some of the leading political figures of the day, including Andrew Jackson, John Quincy Adams, and Abraham Lincoln; military leaders like Ulysses S. Grant, Robert E. Lee, and Thomas "Stonewall" Jackson; and even a few stage performers, among them Edwin Booth and his brother, actor-turned-Lincoln assassin John Wilkes Booth. When the American Civil War broke out in April 1861, Brady decided to leave the studio and use his camera to document the war as it unfolded on the battlefield. Brady received his greatest acclaim for these photos.

Meanwhile, professional photographers in Europe and America were also on the move, capitalizing on an idea that a British photo professional named Francis Frith came up with in the 1850s. Frith traveled the globe taking pictures of places of interest, like the pyramids in Egypt. At the time, drawings were the only way most people could hope to see these wonders of the world. With his images in hand, Frith returned home from his journeys and made a comfortable living selling picture postcards of the most interesting and intriguing places on earth.

The public could not get enough of Frith's postcards, and picture cards produced by other adventurous photographers who ventured to far-off places. No matter how fascinating a building or the mystique of an exotic attraction in one of the world's most remote locations, professional photographers earned the most money taking pictures of people, and that has not changed even to this day.

As far back as 1868, those who made a living with a camera recognized the need to start a professional organization to represent their interests. The organization, the National Photographic Association, officially launched in 1869, represented the concerns of photographers until 1876, when a dwindling membership forced the group to disband. It reorganized as the Professional Photographers of America (PPA) in 1880 and has been promoting picture taking, as well as addressing issues affecting working photographers, ever since.

The 1880s brought other major developments to the world of photography. American businessman and innovator George Eastman revolutionized picture taking in 1884 with the invention of a flexible film that could be used on small rolls. It replaced those clumsy, stiff, glass plates that made taking photos so laborious. Then Eastman introduced a small handheld camera in 1888 specially designed to use his film. The camera made it possible for anyone to take pictures.

That caused concern among professional photographers. They wondered how these cameras would impact the future of those who made a living taking pictures. It soon became evident that there was a big difference between amateurs who owned a camera and professional photographers. The framing, focus, composition, patience, and skill needed to take a photograph that would stand the test of time still required the expertise of a professional photographer.

There was hardly a field in the 20th century that was not affected by professional photography. Everything – including books, magazines, and newspapers – was illustrated with still photographs. Photography was the way to promote or sell anything, and that remains the same in the 21st century.

WHERE YOU WILL WORK

FREELANCE PHOTOGRAPHERS OFTEN WORK out of their homes or rent a small loft or storefront where they can meet with clients and showcase some of their work for the public to see. A professional photographer's workplace can be anywhere. For example, there is an official photographer for the president of the United States, who takes pictures of the chief executive all day long. So that photographer's workplace is the White House or wherever else the president ventures.

Photographers work for corporations, fashion houses, advertising agencies, movie production companies, publishers, magazines, architecture firms, schools, sports teams, car companies, travel agencies, real estate brokerages, and many others. There is no one ideal geographic location, either. In fact, if you live in a warm--weather climate you might get an assignment at the North Pole.

Unpredictability is what makes the job so exciting. Maybe you will be taking pictures at the ballgame one day, be standing with your camera near the red carpet at a movie awards ceremony the next night, and then staking out the runway to photograph the hottest styles at a fashion show. You might even do a few of these assignments all in one day. While you are there, all these locations are your workplace.

As a wildlife photographer, you may be focusing your lens on polar bears in the Arctic Circle one month and camels in the sands of the Sahara a few months later. Nature photographers could be trudging through a rain forest in South America for a few months early in the year and spending the rest of the year high in the Himalayas.

For a product photographer, the perfect setting could be in a studio where you can set up just the right lighting and control the environment to make something your client is selling look tremendously appealing. Maybe you take that product outside, where it is surrounded by people and realistic backgrounds, in natural light.

A wedding photographer may hop on a plane to take pictures at a destination wedding in the Caribbean or just drive a few miles from home to a spectacular old mansion to snap some shots of a bride walking down a picturesque winding staircase to meet her groom.

Fashion photographers stand ankle-deep in sand on a beach taking pictures of models wearing the newest swimsuits. Or you could be knee-high in snow on the slopes photographing this season's must-have skiwear.

The kitchen is the venue for a food photographer whose assignment is snapping images of a celebrity chef's latest creation. You will not be asked to make the food taste delicious, just look delicious. Foodies love to see a vibrant photo of a plate of food next to a recipe listing all the ingredients and instructions on how to make it.

Perhaps you would rather wear a wetsuit than an apron. In that case, consider underwater photography, where your workplace is the sea and your subject matter is everything in it.

Some photographers simply find their material on the street, photographing life as it happens, moving from place to place and capturing the unexpected.

WHAT PHOTOGRAPHERS DO

THE PICTURES TAKEN BY PROFESSIONAL PHOTOGRAPHERS influence people, capture beauty, tell a story, sell a product, preserve history, freeze time, and record life. Your work does not end with snapping photographs. You have to sell your work as well.

Even if you are employed by a company full time taking pictures, and you do not have to worry about where your next paycheck is coming from, you still have to stay at the top of your game, being cutting edge day after day, year after year, to turn out the photos your company needs. As a professional photographer, you must combine creativity, which often showcases the limitless boundaries of imagination, with the reality of the business world.

Whether you own your own studio, work as a freelance photographer, or are employed by a corporation or nonprofit on a full-time basis, your work has to stand out, get noticed.

Technology is an important part of photography, and always has been. Professional photographers have to know about all types of cameras. Today that encompasses both digital and film. Some photographers prefer using film in some cases or might use both digital and film cameras on certain assignments. If you do use film, developing the film and making prints are part of the job. With either film or digital, there will be some editing and touch-up involved to complete the project.

One of your most important tasks is preparation. You need the vision, and advance planning to bring that vision to fruition. You must have the right equipment, make sure it is in working order, have backup equipment, and have an idea of what kind of photos you hope to get, and what it will take to get those shots.

If you are on location, you need to scout out the area and figure out the best place to take your photos. For outdoor shoots, you have to know something about the natural light in the area – how it can work in your favor and how it can work against you. The weather will come into play as well. Indoor photo shoots also require the proper lighting, and, most likely, you will have to bring those lights with you.

If you need help on the assignment, you must have those people lined up in advance and fully briefed on what their jobs entail. If you are using models or actors in the photos, they have to understand both how they fit into the overall project and your concept for the photo shoot.

When the focus of a photo assignment is a product, the setting has to make the product stand out. Understanding what your client wants the photo to convey to the public about the product is vital.

Many photographers choose to specialize. They can usually take any kind of photographs, but prefer to focus on one particular area of picture taking, like wildlife, food, architecture, portraits, or fashion. When you consider the numerous specialties photographers can venture into, you realize what a broad field professional photography is.

The work you do differs to some degree with each area of specialization. In wildlife photography, for example, you can expect to travel the world taking a wide range of photos of animals. The photos can be used for a variety of purposes, including magazines, books, posters, calendars, advertisements, postcards, and museum exhibits.

Certain species of animals are common in only particular parts of the globe and if you want to get their photos in their natural surroundings, you have to go where they are. That might mean spending time in the jungle, the arctic cold, the desert, the rain forest – any place these inhabitants of the wild call home. It could be hours or days before you spot the animal you want to photograph.

Living in your subject's environment can be tough. When you spot the animal you came to take pictures of there is no time to waste. Many photographers study the species of animal they have traveled to photograph so they understand these animals' habits and know what to expect when they encounter them.

Food photography is a hot field today, since cooking is so popular. There are many cookbooks being published, as well as cooking magazines, and all of them are illustrated with photos designed to make your mouth water. You will work with chefs and food stylists to make sure the food is sitting on a plate that accentuates its appeal. Nothing surrounding the food can overpower it. The viewer's eye has to go right to the food. The food has to look fresh and colorful, so if you shoot the dish several times throughout the day, a new portion has to be made for each photo shoot.

Do you want steam rising from a hot plate of food? It is your decision and you only have a short time to get a photo of a steaming-hot meal just right. If you are taking photos of the ingredients, those elements of the recipe must also look top-quality.

The primary considerations in a product shoot is what will make that product look its best? The props around it, the color scheme, and the way it is positioned all must make someone looking at the photo want to reach right in and try the product. Product photography is one of those categories that fits under the umbrella of commercial photography. Anything done for commercial purposes, such as advertising, marketing, public relations, sales, displays, brochures, even menus is considered commercial photography. Your photographs are basically used to sell something.

This type of photography tends to be high-pressure because

you might be asked to take a picture in the afternoon and deliver it that evening. Deadlines may be rigid, but fast service is what can make you valuable. This can be a very lucrative side of the photography business, especially if your photos are driving the sales of your client's product or services.

Creativity counts because you want the public to remember your photo and what it is selling. Fashion photographers are often considered commercial photographers because they have the responsibility of introducing the world to the latest trends in clothing, shoes, and accessories, and getting people to buy and wear these items. This is usually done using photos in paid advertising and sending photos accompanied by press releases to the news media. Working with models is part of the job but the focus of your photographs are the fashions themselves. The tough part of your job is coming up with an original way to present the items in your photographs. To do that, you must understand the idea or concept behind the fashions and take a picture that makes people realize how great that style will look on them.

Portrait photography can be done at a slower pace. Most portraits are taken of an individual or a family. Sometimes a portrait photographer will be called in to take a group shot of an office staff or a graduating class. The challenge is getting all those you photograph – whether an individual, family, or large group – looking their best at the instant when you take the picture. You have to be able to put people at ease, get them to relax, so they do not look stiff or uncomfortable. You want them to forget you are there.

Portrait photographers work out of a studio, but many will also travel to a person's office or home. The ultimate goal is to produce a photo that defines how these people look at this point in their lives.

Usually the calmest person at a wedding is the wedding photographer, but do not let that cool demeanor fool you.

Plenty of stress accompanies the photographing of nuptials. Wedding photographers know that adding to the chaos will only make their job harder. So being the most tranquil person in the room helps the photographer capture everything going on at the happy event without getting in the way. Follow-up is very important in wedding photography, making sure the couple get the photos in a timely fashion and remember to order copies of their favorite pictures to send to family members.

Maybe aerial photography will inspire you. Most photographers do not have their own single-engine planes for aerial photography jobs, so arranging for a plane and pilot for a midair assignment is part of the planning you do. Special cameras are often required as well. Clients who stage an outdoor fair, concert, or similar happening sometimes want aerial photos of the event. The most common use of aerial photography is to study general topography, including mountains, canyons, and valleys, and to get an overview of some acreage before deciding where to start a new development or chart a new highway. Many local and state government officials like to have aerial photographs of a municipality's landmass on file as well.

No area of photography allows you to express yourself more freely than fine art. Fine art photography is the true creative branch of the field. You can take pictures of anything anywhere, color or black and white, there are no boundaries. Many fine art photographers sell their work themselves, though some do sell their pictures through galleries and exhibitions. The work of fine art photographers can also be purchased at craft shows and can be found on display at museums.

Some publications or organizations do not want to spend the money to hire a photographer to take pictures, even though photos are needed. The less expensive alternative is stock photography. Stock photographers take pictures of general subjects, just about anything you can think of. The images are then licensed for specific uses and sold through a stock photograph agency with the photographer getting a royalty. The business is based on volume. Many customers can buy and use the same photo. That translates into a savings for the buyer who did not have to hire a photographer for a photo shoot. Stock photographers usually work as freelancers. Your assignment is to get pictures of something rare and unusual, which is why a professional stock photographer is never seen without a camera.

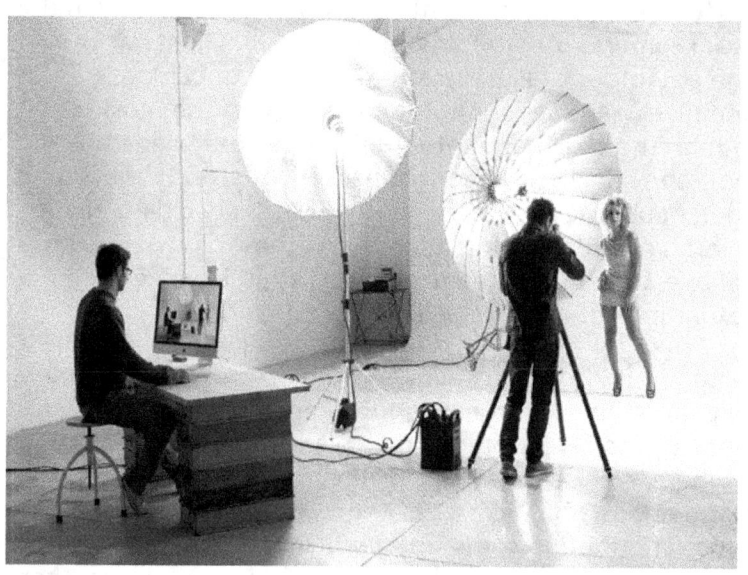

STORIES OF WORKING PHOTOGRAPHERS

I Am a Professional Wildlife Photographer

"Being a professional wildlife photographer is not an easy business to be in, and I emphasize business. I know we are not supposed to be in it for the money and photography is an art form, but if you don't realize that this – or any type of professional photography – is a business, you will simply fail.

Of course, you have to know how to take pictures and be exceptional at it. That goes without saying. However, you have to sell the photos you take and that's where marketing comes in. There are plenty of places to sell your photos. They include wildlife and nature publications and websites, book publishers, travel brochures and websites, calendar publishers, stock picture libraries and agencies, news wire services, galleries, advertising agencies, and many other outlets. I've even sold a couple of my photos to a ceramic company for use on coffee mugs and plates.

You have to line these clients up. They are not going to come to you. Never forget: These are the people who pay so you can travel all over the world to take these photos and afford the equipment, which can be very costly.

This is a very competitive business. Having a good business sense will help you tremendously. I spend more than half my time on the business aspect of photography.

You have to stay in touch with your clients, bring in new clients, constantly sell your work, and provide new creative inventory that's better than whatever else is out there.

I take thousands of pictures a year – sometimes as many as 40,000 to 50,000 or more. You also have to edit, process, and write captions for the photos. You're not going to remember all the details about every photo, so you have to record everything. Then you have to catalog and archive all the photos.

If a client wants certain types of photographs, you have to know where they are and be able to get to them. Say someone wants to see photographs of giraffes. They want to see them now or they will call another photographer. Chances are a potential client might call two or three wildlife photographers around the same time anyway, and if someone else gets the photos to that client first and the client falls in love with those photos, your pictures might not even get looked at.

It has always helped me to study what other wildlife photographers have done and take a different approach so my photos of giraffes, for example, stand out. Take time watching the animal, see if you can capture a pose or a look that isn't ordinary, something people don't normally see. Make your work stand out. It takes time, it takes effort but I find it's well worth it."

I Am a Professional Photographer for a Large Corporation

"You may not even realize a job like mine exists. I work full time as the corporate photographer for a large automobile manufacturer. I spend my time taking pictures of anything you can imagine that has to do with our business, from the latest automobiles the company is putting on the market to corporate executives.

My photos appear everywhere, from internal corporate publications and industry trade periodicals, to those brochures you pick up at the dealership promoting our line of cars, to advertisements and magazine articles. If a picture is needed that has to do with our company, I usually take it.

I've spent weeks taking pictures of workers at our assembly plants. Most people think that when it comes to taking pictures of our cars I do a few photos of the outside of the car and move on to the next thing. In reality, I snap photos of these automobiles from every angle – inside and out. When I take a picture of the interior of the car, I make it feel as though you are sitting in it driving, or how nice it would feel if you were along for the ride. I take hundreds of pictures under the hood.

I have pictures of these cars in different colors, in sunlight, in snow, in rain, at night, near the beach, in the forest. There are pictures of the cars being used for family outings or elegant evenings on the town. There are road shots, garage shots, pictures on city streets, in big driveways, and small ones as well. Once I get done doing all that for a model year, I start all over again when the next year's models come out.

I often go to auto shows and take pictures of our cars, customers, and sales personnel working the exhibit. There are usually some celebrities at these auto shows who stop by to look at the cars and I get photos of them with the cars as well. The real stars of these photos are the cars, not the celebs, so the look on the person's face is very important. The celebrities in the photos have to look drop-dead impressed with the automobile – the wow factor. They have to be drawn to the car, in love with it, dying to take it for a drive, longing to have it, downright overjoyed to be standing next to it. It's my job to get that shot.

On every photo shoot you do, whether it takes a day or week, your job is not complete until you review all the photos you took and make sure you got something really good. Sometimes I will review my work two or three times a day, which is the best aspect of digital equipment – you can find out pretty instantly if you got something you like or you should shoot it again.

It's my job to make the inanimate object I shoot speak to you from the photograph, to have it jump right out of that photo and grab you. I consider that my art."

I Am a Professional Wedding Photographer

"I think wedding photography is one of the most challenging forms of photography. You are capturing once-in-a-lifetime moments in a period of a few hours.

You must stay sharp throughout the entire wedding. There's no time to falter. This work is fast-paced and you must be quick on your feet to keep up with everything that's going on. No two weddings are the same, and the unexpected always happens.

You use all your photography skills each time you shoot a wedding. I'm exhausted both mentally and physically after photographing a wedding. A lot goes into it. It's a demanding job and you are under a considerable amount of pressure.

Wedding photographers have to be able to make adjustments on the fly. You can't stop the action, so you have to be ready to take those pictures when the happy couple walk from sunlight into shade, from inside to outside, or from a well-lit room to a darker room.

The keys to being a good wedding photographer are experience and preparation. You learn from every wedding and that's what gives you the ability to know what to do in every situation. I've done weddings where people wanted photos outside, but it was raining. So you scout out the area, find the settings you would use when the rain lets up or stops for a little while, and have everything ready to go when you get your window of opportunity. Sometimes I can find a gazebo where I can shoot some photos outdoors, even in the rain, or a tree that is so large it shelters the wedding party, even in the rain, and I can get some outside photos.

I meet with the couple several times before the wedding. We exchange ideas. I try to get a list of how many people will be in the group setup shots. I will often go to the wedding site before the big day just to check everything and get familiar with the place. You need to limit the number of surprises you are going to have on the wedding day.

There's always tension at a wedding. I have to be the calmest person in the room. If you are going to be a wedding photographer, you have to know how to work with all types of people who are operating under enormous stress. Normally calm people can be difficult to work with on their wedding day. You have to roll with it. It's nothing personal. You can't let it interfere with the mission at hand.

Sure, you're going to take your setup photos, but your best shots are those fleeting moments that nobody expected. The best smiles, the most touching moments, the most natural-looking pictures, the joy, tears, laughter come in the candid pictures you take, the ones nobody knew you got. That's when people let their emotions show. That's when you get your chance to do your best work and provide people with the picture that will hang on their wall for the rest of their lives. You're watching everything that's going on and you're moving from one location to another, snapping away as you go. I literally try not to miss anything, while not getting in the way of the wedding. It's a neat trick."

PERSONAL QUALITIES

PATIENCE IS A VIRTUE, ESPECIALLY IF YOU are a photographer. Sometimes you have to wait for the sun to set to give you just the right light for the natural effect you want; for a drop of rain to drip off a leaf at a particular angle; or for a mouse to peer out of his hole with that funny, startled look on his face.

Interesting, engaging photographs do not just happen. It takes talent, planning, luck, and patience. The best in this business will tell you that missing an incredible photo because you are too anxious to wait for the ideal moment to shoot is unthinkable.

Good photographers have to be resourceful. How can you get a shot if you really need a ladder to reach the height you want, but you do not happen to have one with you? Is there a balcony nearby? Perhaps standing on the roof of your car might work, or hanging out of a nearby window. You have to be able to come up with a solution. Ingenuity sets the pros apart from the amateurs.

In photography, anticipation is like a sixth sense. Knowing when an awesome photo is merely seconds away, is a gift. It is part of being in the right place at the right time. The ability to anticipate how things are playing out so you can be exactly where you need to be at exactly the right moment is an invaluable trait.

Photography requires great reflexes and excellent eye-hand coordination. Hesitate and you will miss the shot. Creativity is required for success – finding innovative ways to photograph people, places, and things that have been pictured time and time again. That calls for an artistic flair, a vibrant imagination, and an inspired vision.

Ambition, the desire to be the best, will help you succeed. Being a professional photographer is a commercial enterprise, making business savvy important.

Communications skills are vital, too. Photographers who work with people, especially in wedding and fashion shoots, have to gain their confidence and put them at ease. You often have to direct the action, and that means expressing yourself clearly in a calm, friendly manner. When your subjects feel comfortable, you get better photos.

When you are on a photo shoot, you have to remain cool under pressure.

ATTRACTIVE FEATURES

THIS IS A FIELD WHERE IMAGINATION FLOURISHES and thinking outside the box is encouraged. Your creativity will be admired and appreciated.

There are plenty of opportunities to experiment with different techniques, angles, lighting, and all aspects of photography. You can shoot with black and white film, if you want. Your only limitations are getting the job done and meeting your deadline.

This field offers tremendous variety. You will never be bored when you work as a photographer. This is not a mundane, repetitive job. It is different every day, presenting new problems, challenging you to come up with solutions.

Though some photographers specialize in one or a few aspects of photography, you do not have to restrict yourself to a particular category or kind of photography. You can master several specialties, shooting aerial photos one week, sports another, wildlife the week after. Photographers are free to change their specialty, or have no specialty at all.

Rarely do photo opportunities happen in your backyard. If you like to travel, this might be the field for you. Photographers go all over the world to capture the images they need. You might wind up venturing from one destination to another to complete an assignment. You can snap photos on land, at sea, or up in the air. You will not be stuck behind a desk. You are always on the move.

There is plenty of action on a photo shoot. Something is always happening.

Photographers meet many interesting people, providing some wonderful networking opportunities and entrée into intriguing fields. This can lead to additional work, new experiences, and a chance to further your career.

Photographers work behind the scenes. They see fascinating, hidden aspects of different businesses, like the entertainment field.

Photographers always have a chance to get that one-of-a--kind picture – the photo that will come to symbolize an event, evoke the essence of a product, exemplify a travel destination, or represent a generation. You are a visual storyteller, telling that tale through your images.

When you take photographs for a living, you never lack for a way to express yourself. As a photographer, you tap into people's emotions. Your photos can make people happy or sad, elicit joy or anger. You touch people's souls.

UNATTRACTIVE ASPECTS

PHOTOGRAPHIC EQUIPMENT IS VERY EXPENSIVE, especially if you want the latest and greatest gear available. In addition, the technology is constantly changing, so you have to update what is in your camera bag if you want to use state-of-the-art apparatus.

Getting all the newest equipment means you have to learn how to use it. This training is time-consuming. The learning curve can take time away from accepting assignments and earning fees.

Years ago when technology was not changing so rapidly, you could sell some of your old equipment when the time came for an upgrade. Many people were happy to buy good camera equipment secondhand, especially gear that had been used by a professional. That gently used camera gear was more affordable, particularly for those just starting out in the photo business. So it was a win-win for everybody. These days the secondhand market has dwindled, as old devices rely on yesterday's technology.

You may be hired to take photos at a number of exclusive gatherings that most people could only dream about attending. However, you will have very little time to enjoy any of these happenings as you will be running around snapping photos as the event unfolds. There is no time to take it all in, and probably all, except you, will have a good time.

You may get a photo credit for your pictures, but often you do not. If you are looking for recognition, you have to realize that most photographers toil in anonymity. After years of hard work, you have a chance of people getting to know your name and recognizing your work. This is usually reserved for the very best, the top in the field.

Photographers have irregular hours. Being on the job evenings and weekends is commonplace and you will probably have to put in some time behind the lens during holidays. That can be hard on your personal and family life.

Jobs with deadlines are stressful and you feel the pressure until the work gets done.

Steady employment can be hard to find. Many photographers are freelancers, so to keep the paychecks rolling in you will have to put down the camera at times and do some self-promotion. Looking for work can be tedious.

Every photographer has clients who want pictures taken but have only a vague idea of what kind of photos they have in mind. They leave it up to you, but they will be hard to please. You might have to shoot something over and over again – particularly if you are doing a job involving product or commercial photography – until these kinds of clients are satisfied.

EDUCATION AND TRAINING

WHILE A COLLEGE DEGREE IS NOT REQUIRED for most jobs in the photography field, taking some courses after graduating from high school is advisable. It all depends on the type of photography you intend to go into. For instance, if you are thinking of becoming an in-house photographer for a large corporation, the company you are applying to might require a college degree for any full-time employment. If you want to open your own photography studio, most of your customers will probably be more interested in seeing samples of your work than your college diploma, though having some credentials might make you stand out.

In today's digital world, it is essential to know how to use all the newest equipment. You really have to know your camera and your lenses. Understanding exposure, lighting, composition, framing, ISO speed, filters, and how to use editing software is essential. This is the type of education you will get at technical or vocational colleges, as well as many two-year programs at community colleges. These practical programs may serve a professional photographer better than some of the photography programs offered at four-year colleges.

Technical and vocational colleges offer direct-skill training. The photography programs are streamlined, and training is completed in a shorter time – one to two years – rather than four years which is typical for a bachelor's degree.

Technical and vocational colleges expose you to various specialties in the field, like commercial photography, wedding photography, wildlife photography, and many more, giving you the opportunity to experiment to see which area of photography you would like to go into.

At a four-year college, you will learn about photography, but you will also take a variety of other classes, including liberal arts and fine arts, and business and marketing. The focus of the photography degree at many colleges may be more on the artistic aspect of the field, rather than on the commercial facets. You may not start taking classes to perfect your camera skills until your third year in school. On the other hand, your college degree may help you get a job in a different field if photography does not work out for you.

You can always start at a technical or vocational college and pursue a bachelor's degree later on once you get your career going. In addition, at a technical or vocational school with a well-respected photography program, you have an excellent chance of meeting instructors who have a wide range of work experience in photography and are willing to mentor students.

Dakota County Technical College in Rosemount, Minnesota, for example, has four different photography programs. Two of those result in certificates and are designed for students with some experience in the photography field who would like to expand their knowledge of the field. Those programs take a few months to complete. Then there is a one-year diploma program as well as a two-year Associate of Applied Science degree. The associate degree combines photography classes with courses in business. Some of the photography classes offered at DCTC include product photography, location portraits, lighting basics, composition, camera skills, and Photoshop for photographers.

Fortunately, there are many good schools throughout the country that offer classes in photography as well as certificates, diplomas, and degrees in the subject. It will take some research to find the school, either in your area or beyond, that will help you reach your professional goals.

Here are some schools to consider.

Photography School at New York Film Academy

School of the Art Institute of Chicago

New England School of Photography in Boston

Milwaukee Area Technical College School of Media and Creative Arts

California College of the Arts, with campuses in Oakland and San Francisco

---

EARNINGS

THERE IS NO STRAIGHTFORWARD OR SIMPLE ANSWER to the question of how much a professional photographer earns on a yearly basis. Many professional photographers make a good living, but incomes vary greatly.

Professional photographers with studios in New York City or Beverly Hills, for example, can develop a prestige clientele and put a premium price tag on their work. Photographers in small-to medium-sized towns or cities cannot charge close to that. It is fair to say that those with solid experience using a camera, running their own photography business, can earn as much as $75,000 to $90,000 or more annually. Those with their own photography business make more than photographers who work full time for corporations or nonprofits.

At corporations, a staff photographer's income is roughly $60,000 to $65,000 a year, with those working at nonprofits making about $45,000 per year. For photographers with their own business, it comes down to what they can charge for their work. There is no standard answer, and rates are changing all the time. That is why it is always good to be a member of a professional photographers' group and stay in touch with other pros in the field to keep up with the latest trends when it comes to rates.

Some photographers charge by the hour. That rate can start as low as $75 an hour and go as high as $500 an hour. It depends on the job, the type of work involved, as well as where and how the photos will be used. Photographs used in advertising, for instance, command a higher fee than those being taken for a client's personal use.

Some photographers charge by the image. The range can go from $50 a photo to $250 or even more.

You can also charge by assignment or by the job, which photographers normally do when it comes to an event like a party, graduation or wedding. Photographers who make a career out of taking wedding photos usually charge between $2,500 and $3,500 per wedding, but some wedding photographers make as much as $5,000 for taking pictures of the big day. For any professional photographer, annual earnings come down to the volume of your business and how much networking and marketing you do.

OPPORTUNITIES

JUST TAKE A GLIMPSE AROUND YOU. Photographs are everywhere – billboards, advertisements, brochures, magazines, show programs, menus, catalogs, posters, books, the Internet, every place you look. Nothing promotes something or sets a mood like a photo, and people love looking at a good photograph.

The demand for top-notch photography is as strong today as it ever was. Sure, everyone has a cell phone with a camera, but the people taking those pictures are not professional photographers. Most of the images taken on cell phones simply are not very good. Bad photos make people appreciate the great photos taken by talented professionals even more.

Do not buy into the theory that everyone with a cell phone is your competition. Do not be fooled by the premature reports that printed photos are dead. Many print magazines still contain hundreds of photographs and they all have digital editions. Coffee table books with breathtaking photographs are more popular than ever and are considered among the best gifts around.

The ranks of professional photographers continue to swell throughout the United States. The field is expected to grow by 10 percent over the next decade. Work is out there for those who want a career taking photos, but it takes marketing and networking to find it. Those two elements – marketing and networking – are especially important for professional photographers because so many of them are freelancers who own their studios or work from home. That means you have to be a go-getter.

Joining professional organizations, like the Professional Photographers of America (PPA), is one of the best ways to make contacts in the photography business and land jobs. Through these organizations, you can meet photographers who have overflow work and may hire you to help out or recommend you for a job they are too busy to handle. A photographer you become acquainted with at one of these professional groups might be approached about a job outside his/her comfort zone, but knows you would be the perfect person to handle the assignment. That photographer might urge the prospective client to offer you the job instead.

Statewide, nationwide, and international photography

conventions present yet other avenues for you to broaden your connections. They help you get to know professional photographers in far-flung locales and find out about jobs in those regions.

As a photographer, you can always ride a trend to keep your income flow going. For example, if the market for real estate photography, where you have been doing well, suddenly slows down, change your focus and snap some photos in the food or fashion industry for a while. Local business and civic associations, like the chamber of commerce, Rotary Club, or Lions Club, are also great places to network with people in the business world and those in the community who are looking for professional photography.

GETTING STARTED

YOU KNOW YOU CAN TAKE INCREDIBLE PHOTOGRAPHS, but does anyone else know? Getting the word out that you are open for business as a professional photographer will be one of the toughest challenges you will face starting out in this business.

Internships can help. Not only are they an excellent way to break into the field and gain some experience, but you will have a chance to make valuable and lifelong professional contacts. In addition, each of these internships will allow you to explore different aspects of the photography field, from taking wedding pictures, to fashion photos or nature scenes, and perhaps even working a few photo sessions shooting stunning images of high-end consumer products, like expensive jewelry or new automobiles. This work will help you get started on putting together the most important promotional tool you will need to launch your career – an impressive and varied portfolio.

Creating a portfolio starts with the first photos you take. You will want to constantly update this showcase of your artistry with samples of your latest work. Believe it or not, the portfolios you put together in the early days of your career may be the most important because they will get you jobs long before you have a chance to build a reputation in the field. Make up a print and an online version of your portfolio.

Try to get your work in the public eye. Many places in the community will be more than happy to dress up their empty walls by putting your photographs on display. People in charge of local libraries, community centers, town halls, theaters, and restaurants may all be open to the idea of giving professional photographers just starting out some wall space for an exhibition. Once your photos are on display, do not forget to let the local news media know where people can view your photos.

A website is a natural for photographers and gives you unlimited space to present not only your best pictures but your personal favorites as well. You will also have room to talk about your work and discuss your philosophy about professional picture taking.

When you are breaking into the field of professional photography, there is no such thing as a small job. You never know where you will meet someone who will give you your next job or introduce you to a person who eventually turns into one of your most lucrative clients.

Never assume that an organization has a professional photographer on the job. Just because businesses, nonprofits, tourist destinations, and other organizations give out brochures and information featuring photographs does not mean they have a photographer working for them or, if they do, that they are happy with that photographer. Approach all those you might think could use your services – you might be just who they are looking for.

ASSOCIATIONS

■ **Professional Photographers of America (PPA)**
http://www.ppa.com

■ **Photographic Society of America (PSA)**
https://psa-photo.org

■ **North American Nature Photography Association (NANPA)**
http://www.nanpa.org

■ **Association of International Photography Art Dealers (AIPAD)**
http://www.aipad.com

■ **Wedding and Portrait Photographers International (WPPI)**
www.wppionline.com

■ **Wedding Photojournalist Association (WPJA)**
https://www.wpja.com

■ **The Association of Independent Architectural Photographers (AIAP)**
http://www.aiap.net

■ **International Freelance Photographers Organization (IFPO)**
http://www.aipress.com

■ **American Photographic Artists (APA)**
http://apanational.org

■ American Society of Media Photographers (ASMP)
https://www.asmp.org

SCHOOLS

■ Dakota County Technical College
http://www.dctc.edu/academics/programs-majors/
design-careers/photographic-imaging
-technology

■ Photography School at New York Film Academy, headquartered in New York City with campuses around the world
https://www.nyfa.edu/photography-school

■ School of the Art Institute of Chicago
http://www.saic.edu/academics
/departments/photography

■ New England School of Photography in Boston,
http://www.nesop.edu

■ Milwaukee Area Technical College School of Media and Creative Arts
http://www.matc.edu/media_creative_arts/degrees
/photography.cfm

■ California College of the Arts, with campuses in Oakland and San Francisco
https://www.cca.edu/academics/photography

WEBSITES

■ **American Society of Picture Professionals (ASPP)**
http://aspp.com

■ **The Imaging Alliance**
www.theimagingalliance.com

■ **Women in Photography International**
http://womeninphotography.org/wipihome.html

■ **Society for Photographic Education (SPE)**
https://www.spenational.org

■ **Stock Artists Alliance (SAA)**
http://www.photometadata.org

■ **American Photo**
www.americanphotomag.com

■ **Fstoppers**
https://fstoppers.com

■ **DPReview**
https://www.dpreview.com

■ **PetaPixel**
https://petapixel.com

■ **Kenkaminesky.com**
www.kenkaminesky.com/index

■ **Light Stalking**
https://www.lightstalking.com

■ **The Phoblographer**
http://www.thephoblographer.com

■ Museum of Photographic Arts
https://mopa.org

Institute For Career Research CHICAGO

CAREERS INTERNET DATABASE
www.careers-inter net.org